THE VALUE OF GIVING

The Story of Beethoven

VALUE COMMUNICATIONS, INC.
PUBLISHERS
LA JOLLA, CALIFORNIA

THE VALUE OF GIVING

The Story of
Beethoven

BY ANN DONEGAN JOHNSON

THE DANBURY PRESS

The Value of Giving is part of the ValueTales series.

The Value of Giving text copyright © 1979 by Ann Donegan Johnson. Illustrations copyright © 1979 by Value Communications, Inc.
All rights reserved under International and Pan American Copyright Conventions.
No part of this book may be reproduced in any manner whatsoever without written permission from the publisher, except in the case of brief quotations embodied in reviews and articles.

First Edition
Manufactured in the United States of America
For information write to: ValueTales, P.O. Box 1012
La Jolla, CA 92038

Library of Congress Cataloging in Publication Data

Johnson, Ann Donegan.
    The value of giving.

    (ValueTales)
    SUMMARY: A brief biography of Ludwig van Beethoven, emphasizing the importance of giving in his life.
    1. Beethoven, Ludwig van, 1770-1827—Juvenile literature. 2. Composers—Germany—Biography—Juvenile literature. [1. Beethoven, Ludwig van, 1770-1827. 2. Composers] I. Title.
ML3930.B4J6   780'.92'4 [B] [92]   78-31545

ISBN 0-916392-34-1

Dedicated to Betty
who gave me her support
when I needed it.

This tale is about a gifted person, Ludwig van Beethoven. The story that follows is based on events in his life. More historical facts about Beethoven can be found on page 63.

Once upon a time...

long, long ago, in the German city of Bonn, a little boy was born to a couple named Beethoven.

"It's almost Christmas time," said the child's mother, Maria, as she held the baby close. "What a wonderful present we have! Isn't he beautiful?"

But the baby's father, Jan van Beethoven, wasn't nearly so happy. "He's an ugly baby, if you ask me," said Jan, and he went off to join his friends at the tavern.

"Never mind," Maria whispered to the little one. "I think you're a lovely baby."

Just then, Jan's father came bustling into the room.

"Wonderful! Wonderful!" he cried, when he saw his new grandson. "You mark my words, Maria. This boy will be a fine musician some day."

Maria smiled. "Like you?" she said. "And like his father?"

Grandfather Beethoven looked unhappy then. He did not like to think too much about Jan. Jan could have been a marvelous singer, but he wasted his days at the tavern with his ne'er-do-well friends.

Maria had named the baby Ludwig, after his grandfather, and as time went by she gave him the things a good mother gives to her child. She gave him tenderness and care and love.

Soon Maria noticed that Ludwig wasn't quite like other little boys. He heard things that most children never noticed. He clapped his hands with delight when the church bells rang out. He laughed at the murmur the River Rhine made as it flowed past the city.

One day, when Maria was busy with her housework, little Ludwig found the front door open. He looked out at the narrow, cobbled street that ran past the house.

"I wonder what's at the end of the street," said Ludwig to himself, and he decided to go and see. He trotted out the door and down the street, and he walked and walked until he came to an open field.

It was beautiful in the field, and very peaceful. Ludwig sat down in a soft, grassy spot and he listened. He heard birds singing. He heard wind rustling the leaves of the trees. He heard a faint tinkling of cowbells off in the distance.

Ludwig was very young, of course, but he already knew about music. And it seemed to him that all the music in the world must have started with the sounds of nature—the sounds of wind stirring green leaves and of birds singing.

10

While his mother gave Ludwig love and tenderness, his grandfather gave him some wonderful adventures. Every day the old man and the child explored the city of Bonn, and on one very special day Grandfather took Ludwig to the chapel where the archbishop went to pray.

"It's very beautiful!" said Ludwig, when they were inside.

"Yes it is," said Grandfather, "but you musn't talk in church. It's forbidden."

Grandfather then led Ludwig to a seat and they waited. And suddenly the church was filled with a most wonderful sound.

"Grandfather, what is it?" whispered Ludwig.

"It's the organ," his grandfather answered.

Just then a rich tenor voice rang out.

"And that is your father," said Grandfather Beethoven. His voice was sad, for the thought of his son idling away his life in the tavern always made him bitter. "He could be a great musician," said the grandfather, "if only he weren't such a wastrel."

As Ludwig grew bigger, he and his grandfather often went far beyond the streets of the city. They took long, rambling walks through the fields and the valleys around Bonn, and they talked about nature and about music. Sometimes when they were tired of walking, they rode a boat down the River Rhine.

"Will we always be together?" Ludwig asked his grandfather. "Will you always take me to see wonderful things and to listen to beautiful music?"

Grandfather didn't answer, and before long a day came that was different from any Ludwig had known.

Ludwig was playing by himself when he realized that the house was very quiet.

"Something's the matter," said the boy. "Mother has gone out somewhere. And Grandfather hasn't come to take me for our walk. I'll go to Grandfather's house. Perhaps Mother is there."

Indeed, when Ludwig reached the cottage where his grandfather lived, his mother was there. His father was there, too, and he looked very serious.

"Poor little fellow," said his mother. She put her arms around Ludwig. "Your grandfather has died," she told him.

After that, Ludwig was very lonely. He still walked in the fields and listened to the birds singing, but it was not the same now.

"I wish Grandfather were still here," thought Ludwig. "Perhaps if I had a little friend it would help."

One day Ludwig couldn't go to the fields because it was raining. He wandered through the house and came across a curious box that his father had brought home.

"I wonder what's in it," said Ludwig to himself.

He looked around to see if anyone was watching. Then he lifted the lid—and out hopped a strange little cat, a cat who laughed and capered and told Ludwig that his name was Keys. "Just like the keys on a piano," said the cat. "Or the keys on this instrument."

Ludwig was delighted. His wish had come true. He had a little playmate. "I know I made you up," he told the cat, "but I'm going to keep you as my friend. I need a friend."

"Indeed you do," said the cat. "And now that that's settled, why don't you try this instrument?"

So Ludwig touched the keys on the instrument, and the room was filled with beautiful sounds. "It's wonderful!" cried Ludwig. "When I play at one end, it sounds like birds chirping. At the other end, it sounds like thunder."

But then Ludwig heard someone behind him. He turned around, and he began to tremble.

Who do you suppose was there?

19

It was Ludwig's father, standing in the doorway.

Poor Ludwig was terrified. "I'm sorry, Father," he said. "I just wondered what was in the box you brought home, and such beautiful sounds came out when I touched the keys that I couldn't stop."

For once, Jan van Beethoven didn't shout or scold. "That is called a clavier," he said quietly, and he sat down and began to play.

Ludwig listened. At first the music gave him a peaceful feeling. Then it grew livelier and it excited him. And sometimes it made him feel sad.

When Jan stopped playing, he turned to Ludwig. "Would you like to learn how to do it?" he asked.

"Could I really?" cried Ludwig.

"I don't see why not," said Jan. "I will teach you."

21

Ludwig's mother came home that day and found Jan teaching Ludwig to play the clavier.

"Look, Mother!" cried Ludwig. "Father is giving me lessons!"

"Oh, that's grand!" cried his mother. "Jan, it warms my heart to see you giving your time to your son."

Jan smiled a secret smile. He was thinking of a young musician named Mozart who had become a famous pianist and composer at the age of nine. "Mozart was a child prodigy, and he made lots of money," thought Jan. "I will make sure that Ludwig becomes a prodigy, too—and he can make money for me!"

Poor little Ludwig. His father was not the giving sort. Quite the opposite. Jan van Beethoven intended to take all that he could from the child.

Ludwig learned quickly. Every time the boy played, Jan dreamed of the money Ludwig might make. Soon he was forcing Ludwig to practice long hours.

"Please, Father," said Ludwig one day. "I love the music, but I'm tired right now. Can't I rest for a bit?"

"You can rest when we're rich!" shouted his father. "Right now you can practice!" And he brought a stick down on Ludwig's hands.

"Jan, stop!" cried Ludwig's mother. "You'll hurt him!"

"He'll be a great musician!" shouted Jan. "He'll make heaps of money. Now stop sniveling, Ludwig! To work!"

In spite of the shouting and the rages and the weariness, Ludwig did love the music. When his father wasn't at home, he sometimes played just for himself and Keys.

In a few years Ludwig had learned everything that his father could teach him, and he began to make a little money playing in the homes of the wealthy people of Bonn.

"It isn't much," he told Keys, "but it gives me a chance to play in front of people. And if Father doesn't spend it all at the tavern, perhaps I can buy some nice things for Mother."

Ludwig was about ten when his father came home one night and brought a friend with him. The man's name was Tobias, and he had once been a great musician in Frankfurt. Tobias was like Jan, however. He spent too much time in the tavern.

"Get up, Ludwig!" bellowed Jan. "Tobias has come to hear you play!"

Ludwig didn't argue when his father shouted that way. He tumbled out of bed, and so did Keys.

27

"Very good!" said Tobias when he heard Ludwig play. "The boy has talent. I will give him lessons."

And Tobias began to teach Ludwig. Tobias was a better musician than Jan, and a finer teacher. But he never started his lessons with Ludwig until the tavern was closed. Then he came roaring in and Jan made Ludwig get out of bed and play for him.

"Be brave, Ludwig," whispered Keys. "Forget that you are sleepy. Just think of the music and it will be all right."

Ludwig's mother cried when Jan shouted at the boy, but she couldn't stop her husband. She couldn't do much about her two younger sons, either. They liked to tease Ludwig about his looks. They told him that he was ugly and that dogs barked at him when he walked down the street.

"Don't pay any attention," said Keys. "Looks aren't important. When you become a great musician, that is what people will see—only your greatness!"

Ludwig tried to believe what Keys said to him, and before long he had such a stroke of luck that he thought it might really come true.

An excellent musician named Christian Gottlob Neefe heard Ludwig play, and he was impressed. "You show promise," said Neefe. "You still have much to learn, of course. I will give you lessons. And I would like to teach you to compose."

"I have already composed some little pieces," said Ludwig, and he played them for Herr Neefe.

"Excellent!" said Neefe. "In time you should be really good!"

Ludwig was delighted, and so was Keys. Of course Ludwig enjoyed the company of his small friend, so he kept the little cat with him while he practiced every day. He no longer practiced at home on the clavier. Now he played the organ in a church. And Keys was there the day Neefe came to announce that Ludwig was to play for the Elector.

Now in those days the Elector wasn't quite as important as a king or an emperor, but he *was* important. He was the ruler of the area where Ludwig lived, and when Ludwig heard that he was to go to court and play for this man, he was terribly excited.

"Mother, I cannot believe it," he said. "I'm so nervous!"

32

"You'll do well," said his mother. "I know you will."

Even Ludwig's father was pleased. At last, he thought, Ludwig would be well-known, and he would make lots of money. So Jan bought Ludwig a fine satin coat, and he sent the boy to court.

Ludwig was dazzled at first. He saw the chandeliers sparkling overhead and the mirrors everywhere. He saw the elegant people crowding the ballroom, and the Elector sitting in the front of the audience.

"Oh, Keys!" he whispered. "My legs are shaking. I don't think I can walk to the clavier!"

"Of course you can walk to the clavier!" said Keys. "Just think of the music! You never fail when you think only of the music!"

Ludwig went to the instrument. He sat down, and his hands were trembling when he began to play. But once he heard the notes coming from the Elector's marvelous clavier—which was so much better than the old one at home—Ludwig forgot to be nervous. Keys was right. Ludwig could not fail when he forgot everyone and everything but the music.

There was silence for an instant when Ludwig finished playing. Then the audience began to applaud. "Bravo! Bravo!" cried the courtiers.

"You did it!" cried Keys. "Ludwig, you did it! Look! Even the Elector is clapping!"

"I've been so fortunate," said Ludwig to Keys when the great day was over. "People have given me so much—lessons, a place to practice, a chance to play at court!"

"Keep working," said Keys, "and some day you will have a chance to repay all those gifts."

So Ludwig went on practicing and composing. Then one day Neefe arrived with the word that he was to play the clavier in the court orchestra.

"It doesn't pay much," said Neefe, "but it's a great honor."

"Honor?" shouted Jan van Beethoven when Ludwig told him the news. "Who cares about honor? Money! That's what counts!"

"But it's a great opportunity!" cried Ludwig.

"Ugly fellows like you need every opportunity that comes their way," said his brothers.

"Never mind, Ludwig," said his mother. "You are not ugly, and you must go ahead and take the position. I'm proud of you!"

Ludwig did take the position, and soon he was made assistant court organist—which paid more. But Ludwig didn't want to stay in Bonn forever—not even as court organist.

"There is still so much I don't know," he told Keys. "I want to go to Vienna and study with the great masters."

Ludwig began to save what money he could. And when he was seventeen he took all that he had saved, and some money he borrowed, and he told his mother that he was going to Vienna.

"That's . . . that's wonderful, Ludwig," said his mother. She wanted him to have his chance to be a great musician, but she would miss him very much. She tried not to show that she was sad as he set off for Vienna, carrying a letter from the Elector to the great composer Mozart.

"Not many people get a chance to play for Mozart," said Keys, for of course the cat went to Vienna, too.

"I am a very lucky young man," said Ludwig. "I am also a very nervous young man."

"Very well, sir," said Mozart, when Ludwig presented himself and his letter. "Let me hear what you can do."

Ludwig sat down at the piano and he began to play. And it was like his performance at court; the moment the music began, Ludwig forgot to be nervous.

"You play well," said Mozart when Ludwig finished. "I would like you to stay in Vienna. I would like to teach you."

Mozart not only taught Ludwig, he also saw to it that the boy met other musicians. Ludwig had a wonderful time talking to gifted people and going to fine concerts.

"One day I'll bring my mother to Vienna," Ludwig told Keys. "I'll take her to see the sights, and I'll give her all sorts of beautiful things."

"You should," said Keys. "Look at everything she's given you."

But even while Ludwig was dreaming of the fine time he would have with his mother, a letter arrived at the inn where he was staying. Ludwig opened the letter and felt a great sadness.

"My mother is very ill," he told Keys. "I must go home right away."

Ludwig hurried back to Bonn, and not long after he arrived, his mother died.

Now, for the first time in his life, music failed to comfort Ludwig. His mother had been the one person who had always given him love, and now she was gone. Ludwig went to the cathedral to practice every day, but he went as if he were walking in his sleep. On his way he passed a beautiful garden filled with flowers and trees, and sometimes he and Keys sat there and rested and thought of his mother.

Ludwig was sitting in the garden one day when he heard a soft voice say, "Is something the matter?"

Ludwig turned to see a lady standing in the garden.

"You look so sad," said the lady. "My name is Frau von Breuning and this is my garden. Tell me what's troubling you."

The lady looked kind, so Ludwig told her about his mother.

"I understand," said Frau von Breuning. "My dear husband passed away not long ago, and I felt a great sadness. Why don't you come and meet my children and stay for supper with us?"

Ludwig was happy not to have to go home to his own cheerless house. He was glad to meet Frau von Breuning's four children, and he was pleased that they seemed to take a liking to him. "Welcome, Ludwig!" they cried, and they showed him into the dining room.

"What nice people!" said Keys, who watched as they laughed and chatted during supper.

Ludwig had not been so happy since he left Vienna, and when Frau von Breuning heard that he was a musician, she insisted that he play for them.

Ludwig did play, and for the first time in months he felt joyful about his music.

"Ah!" said Keys. "That sounds like my friend Ludwig again!"

"How very beautiful!" said Frau von Breuning, and she and her children offered Ludwig their friendship—a friendship that was to last a lifetime.

Ludwig found new courage after that evening with the Breunings. He worked with fresh inspiration at his composing. And in the days that followed he met a man named Count von Waldstein.

The count was very rich, and he loved music. He was greatly impressed with Ludwig, and one day he decided that he would visit the young man at his home and surprise him.

It was indeed a surprise! The count found Ludwig living in a shabby house on a mean little street. His room was dark and untidy, with sheets of music scattered over the floor. A battered piano was stuck back in the corner, and Ludwig was hunched over this, working on his newest composition.

"What a disgrace!" said the count to himself. "Ludwig van Beethoven is a fine musician. He shouldn't have to use such a dreadful old instrument!"

Ludwig looked up then, and he saw the count. He leaped to his feet and invited his guest to sit down. He tried to pretend that everything was all right, but he was terribly embarrassed.

"I'm glad we don't have lots of company," said Keys. "It *is* messy in here!"

A few days later, two husky men called upon Ludwig—and delivered a beautiful new piano.

"For me?" Ludwig was quite stunned at the sight of the marvelous instrument. "But there must be some mistake. I didn't order a piano—and I have no money to pay for one!"

"It's a gift," said one of the men, "from the Count von Waldstein."

Of course Ludwig was thrilled. And he soon learned that there were other surprises in store for him. Count von Waldstein saw to that—and so did the Elector.

First, Franz Joseph Haydn, a truly great musician, visited the Elector, and Ludwig had a chance to play for him. Then, when Haydn offered to give Ludwig lessons, Count von Waldstein sent Ludwig off to Vienna so that he could study with him. What is more, he made sure Ludwig had enough money to live while he was there!

Ludwig started his lessons with Haydn as soon as he was settled in Vienna. Soon other great musicians learned about Ludwig, and they offered to share their knowledge with the young man.

"So many people are generous with me," said Ludwig to himself. "The least I can do is give something to those who need it." So, when he could, Ludwig sent money to his father and his brothers, who were at home in Bonn.

Soon Ludwig was giving more than money. He was giving pleasure to many people, for those who heard of his music came from far and near to listen to him play.

"Bravo!" they would shout. "Encore! Play more, Beethoven!"

But then, just when everything was going so well for Ludwig, a very sad thing happened.

It started gradually. At first Beethoven wasn't even sure about it. "It may be my imagination," he said to Keys, "but I don't seem to hear as well as I used to."

"Not hear well?" said Keys. "But that's terrible! You must go to see a doctor right away!"

Ludwig did go to see a doctor. He went to see many doctors. They looked sad and they shook their heads. "Sorry, Herr van Beethoven," they said, "but there is nothing we can do. In time you will be completely deaf."

"Keys, what will happen to me?" cried Ludwig. "I am only thirty years old. I have hardly started my work. What will I do?"

Poor little Keys didn't know the answer. Each day Ludwig's hearing grew worse. At last Ludwig couldn't hear the piano any more. The only thing he could hear was Keys—and that was because Keys was in his own imagination.

"Keep trying," Keys would say. "Please, keep trying."

But it was so hard. Ludwig could not imagine his life without music. He became terribly depressed. He wouldn't go out of the house and he wouldn't let his friends come to see him.

"Come now, Ludwig," said Keys at last. "Are you going to sit and feel sorry for yourself for the rest of your life? So many people have given so much to help you develop your talents. Perhaps it's time you gave something back!"

Then Ludwig remembered the love he had had from his mother, and the adventures with his grandfather. He recalled the lessons he had had from his father's friend Tobias, and from Herr Neefe. "And the Elector has been good to me," he said to Keys. "And Frau von Breuning and Mozart and Haydn and Count von Waldstein. You are right. They have given me so much. I can't let it go to waste!"

Soon Ludwig's friends heard that he was composing again.

"I can do it!" he said to Keys. "I can hear the music in my mind—and it is good!"

"I told you so!" cried Keys. "And it *is* beautiful! It's the most beautiful music you ever wrote!"

Some people have said that the music Beethoven wrote after he became deaf is the most beautiful music *anyone* has ever written.

"You should be happier now," said Keys. "You are giving your gifts to the world."

"It's certainly better than brooding," said Ludwig. "But there is one thing I would like to do, and I'm not sure I can do it. I would like to conduct my Ninth Symphony."

People were startled when they heard about this—and they were not encouraging. "How can you conduct an orchestra if you cannot hear the music?" said some of Ludwig's friends. "Better to forget it."

"Don't pay any attention to them, Ludwig," whispered Keys. "Lots of people thought you couldn't compose, either, after you lost your hearing."

"And I did, didn't I?" said Ludwig. "So I will conduct."

But when Ludwig stood up in front of the orchestra, the musicians were very, very nervous.

They watched as Ludwig signaled for the symphony to begin. Their eyes were on him as they began to play. And the music was so clear in Ludwig's mind that he conducted beautifully.

The music went on and on, and Ludwig knew every note. He and the orchestra performed together like one marvelously tuned instrument. At that moment there was nothing for Ludwig but his symphony. And then it was over.

Ludwig stood still facing the orchestra. Now that there was no more music, there was silence for him. But then one of the musicians came to him and turned him around so that he faced the audience. He saw that everyone was standing and clapping. He saw that some people cheered and others wept with delight.

"You were wonderful!" whispered Keys. "You've given the world something that will last forever."

And Keys was right. Beethoven's music is so beautiful that people enjoy it today as much as they did then.

Of course not everyone can give the world great music, as Beethoven did. But sooner or later, everyone has the opportunity to give something to make someone else happier. Your gifts may be very simple, but if they make someone else happy, you will probably be happier, too.

And if someone gives you a gift—a gift of time or money or attention—try to receive it with joy. It's more fun that way for the one who is giving the gift—and more fun for you, too. Giving is like lots of other valuable things; it has to work both ways.

The End

Historical Facts

Ludwig van Beethoven was born into a musical family on December 16, 1770, in Bonn, Germany. His grandfather was the director of the court orchestra and his father was a singer in the royal choir. He lived in poverty, however, because his father preferred drinking over working to support his family.

As a young child, Beethoven developed a passion for the outdoors that was to last a lifetime. He took great pleasure in listening to the sound of the wind as it stirred the trees, to the songs of the birds, and to the murmuring of the River Rhine as it flowed downstream. Early on, he felt that the true source of music was Nature.

His musical training began when he was four years old. Recognizing Ludwig's musical talent, his father, Jan, had hopes that Ludwig could use his talent to earn money to support the family. Eager for the boy to learn quickly, Jan often beat him into practicing more and more. One day, Ludwig's mother, Maria-Magdalena, tried to intervene. Jan began to beat her with a strap. Ludwig begged his father to stop. This upset the boy so much that from that day forward Ludwig never had to be encouraged to practice. He wanted to learn all that he could so that someday he could give his beloved mother the beautiful things he felt she deserved.

It was not long before Beethoven began composing his own music. By 1782, some of his compositions were published. In 1787, he traveled to Vienna where he met and performed for Mozart. After listening to Beethoven play, Mozart commented to his friends, "Keep your eyes on him. Someday, he will give the world something to talk about." Indeed, this prophecy came true.

Beethoven studied with many of the great musical masters. But he felt restricted by the rules of composition set by his teachers. He longed to write music with a freer, more modern interpretation than was being written in the

LUDWIG VAN BEETHOVEN
(1770–1827)

early 1800s. By the time Beethoven wrote his Third Symphony, he had established his identity as a truly original composer.

In 1798, Beethoven began to lose his hearing. During the years that followed, his despondency at not being able to hear the music drove him into moods of deep depression and eccentricity. But he continued to compose. In his lifetime, he produced nine symphonies, five piano concertos, thirty-two piano sonatas, sixteen string quartets, an opera, a mass, a ballet, and seventy unnumbered compositions.

His Ninth Symphony was finished in 1823, when he was totally deaf. Nevertheless, Beethoven conducted the first performance of this work. When the symphony was over, a soloist in the orchestra took him by the arm and turned him around so that he could see the audience clapping wildly. Smiling at them he said, "I write not for you, but for those who shall come after."

Three years later, on March 26, 1827, Beethoven died of pneumonia. But he left the world a most wonderful gift—his glorious music that is shared by all of us.

Other Titles in the ValueTale Series

THE VALUE OF BELIEVING IN YOURSELF	The Story of Louis Pasteur
THE VALUE OF DETERMINATION	The Story of Helen Keller
THE VALUE OF PATIENCE	The Story of the Wright Brothers
THE VALUE OF KINDNESS	The Story of Elizabeth Fry
THE VALUE OF HUMOR	The Story of Will Rogers
THE VALUE OF TRUTH AND TRUST	The Story of Cochise
THE VALUE OF CARING	The Story of Eleanor Roosevelt
THE VALUE OF COURAGE	The Story of Jackie Robinson
THE VALUE OF CURIOSITY	The Story of Christopher Columbus
THE VALUE OF RESPECT	The Story of Abraham Lincoln
THE VALUE OF IMAGINATION	The Story of Charles Dickens
THE VALUE OF FAIRNESS	The Story of Nellie Bly
THE VALUE OF SAVING	The Story of Benjamin Franklin
THE VALUE OF LEARNING	The Story of Marie Curie
THE VALUE OF SHARING	The Story of the Mayo Brothers
THE VALUE OF RESPONSIBILITY	The Story of Ralph Bunche
THE VALUE OF HONESTY	The Story of Confucius
THE VALUE OF UNDERSTANDING	The Story of Margaret Mead
THE VALUE OF LOVE	The Story of Johnny Appleseed
THE VALUE OF FANTASY	The Story of Hans Christian Andersen
THE VALUE OF FORESIGHT	The Story of Thomas Jefferson
THE VALUE OF HELPING	The Story of Harriet Tubman
THE VALUE OF DEDICATION	The Story of Albert Schweitzer
THE VALUE OF FRIENDSHIP	The Story of Jane Addams

Value Tales™